Best Bacon Infused Dessert Recipes

\

20 Mouthwatering Delicious Desserts Infused with Bacon

Diana Loera

Other Books by Diana Loera

12 Extra Special Summer Dessert Fondue Recipes http://tinyurl.com/q7gpgw8

Fast Start Guide to Flea Market selling http://tinyurl.com/qb83smw

14 Extra Special Winter Holidays Fondue Recipes http://tinyurl.com/lkebggx

Awesome Thanksgiving Leftovers Revive Guide http://tinyurl.com/prxjayg

Stop Hot Flashes now http://tinyurl.com/kxmr8ps

Party Time Chicken Wing Recipes   http://tinyurl.com/ohsc9x8

Summertime Sangria   http://tinyurl.com/oxnlnhm

Please visit www.LoeraPublishingLLC.com to see our complete selection of books.
Topics include cooking, travel, recipes, how to, non- fiction and more.

You're also invited to visit www.Swingbellys.com to see the complete selection of my recipe books.

Introduction

Thank you for taking the time to read this book. I enjoy researching a wide variety of topics and creating books.

Due to the ongoing bacon craze and bacon lovers in my family, I decided to publish bacon infused recipes.

Several people mentioned that the bacon infused desserts were a family favorite. With that info in mind, I started going through recipes to select the best of the best recipes.

I then created this book focusing on the top bacon infused desserts.

While all of these recipes can be made year around, there are some that really appeal to me as fall recipes.

I also included a bacon maple marshmallow recipe that I think would be fun to make with kids as most of us just grab a bag of marshmallows at the grocery store.

It was cool to actually make marshmallows although, the recipe is one that is a bit time consuming. It does make the perfect Saturday afternoon or school break recipe.

I hope that you enjoy these recipes as much as I enjoyed finding, testing and sharing them with you.

With all of my books I publish the softcover version in the larger 8 ½ x 11 size. I don't like squinting at small font and don't want to ask you to do it either.

I also like to include color photos showcasing some recipes.

Each photo that I add drives the publishing cost up so I have to be selective regarding photos – thank you for understanding.

As my granddaughter has nut allergies, I like to mention to readers – please check with guests for any food allergies – such as nut allergies – before serving these recipes. Some do contain nuts.

I also included a couple recipes that are gluten free versions. While I like eating gluten free, I don't have too yet there are many people who must adhere to a gluten free diet. I wanted to include gluten free recipes in this book in case you have someone in your family who follows a gluten free diet.

Table of Contents

Bacon Maple Apple Crisp

Ingredients:

Topping

6 slices of bacon cut into 1/4 inch pieces

3/4 cup Bob's Red Mill Gluten Free all-purpose flour

3/4 cup pecans, chopped fine

3/4 cup Gluten Free rolled oats

1/2 cup organic whole brown sugar

1/4 cup granulated white sugar

1/2 teaspoon ground cinnamon

1/2 teaspoon salt

1 stick (8 Tbsp.) butter, melted

Filling:

9 small Gala apples (or 7 medium size apples of your choice) peeled, cored, halved and cut into 1/2 inch wedges

1/3 cup pure maple syrup

1 cup apple cider

1 Tbsp. fresh squeezed lemon juice

2 Tbsp. butter

Directions:

1. Preheat oven to 450° with the oven rack in middle.

2. Cook bacon in a skillet over medium heat until crisp. Drain on paper towels.

3. Combine flour with the pecans, oats, sugars, cinnamon and salt in a medium bowl. Stir in the melted butter until everything is moist but crumbly and then stir in the bacon pieces. Set aside.

Filling

4. Toss your apple wedges with the maple syrup and set aside.

5. Bring the cider to a simmer in a clean 12″ skillet and reduce by half. (about 5 minutes), transfer to a bowl, add the lemon juice, stir and set aside.

6. Melt the butter in your now empty 12 inch skillet on medium heat. When it stops foaming add the apples tossed in maple syrup. Cook for about 14 minutes. stirring frequently. Don't fully cook the apples. Remove from heat and stir in the reduced apple cider/lemon juice mixture.

7. Distribute the topping evenly over the top of the apples. Place the skillet on a baking sheet in the oven and bake for 15 to 20 minutes. You will want the topping to look golden brown.

Cool on a wire rack for 15 minutes and serve. Ice cream or whipped cream makes a great addition to this recipe.

Maple Bacon Apple Crisp

Maple Caramel Pumpkin Cake with Bacon Crumble Topping

Candied Maple Bacon

8 strips of maple bacon

4 tablespoons maple sugar

Pumpkin Cake

2 cups all-purpose flour

1 teaspoon baking soda

1 teaspoon ground cinnamon

1/2 teaspoon table salt

14 oz. can pumpkin puree

1/2 cup granulated sugar

1/2 cup packed brown sugar

1 egg

1/4 cup (1/2 stick) unsalted butter, melted

1 teaspoon vanilla

1/4 cup chopped, toasted pecans

Maple Caramel Frosting

1 cup (2 sticks) unsalted butter

2 cups packed brown sugar

1/2 teaspoon salt

1 cup pure maple syrup

4 oz. cream cheese, cut into 4 cubes

Optional

Fleur de sel

Directions

1.Bacon: Preheat oven to 400°F. Line rimmed baking sheet with foil. Place a metal rack on foil.

2.Lay bacon slices on rack. Sprinkle 2 tablespoons maple sugar evenly over bacon.

3.Bake until sugar is melted, about 8 minutes. Sprinkle remaining 2 tablespoon sugar over same side of bacon. Bake until bacon is deep brown and glazed, 12 to 14 minutes longer. Remove from oven.

4. Preheat broiler. Broil bacon until sugar bubbles, watching closely so that it won't burn. 1-2 minutes is all that is needed. Let bacon cool on rack and then dice.

5.Cake: Preheat oven to 350°F. Coat a 9 x 13 baking pan with nonstick spray.

6.Whisk together flour, baking soda, cinnamon and table salt for the bars in a medium bowl; set aside. Whisk together pumpkin puree, granulated sugar, 1/2 cup brown sugar, egg, melted butter and vanilla in a large bowl until well blended. Stir in flour mixture and pecans.

7.Spread pumpkin batter evenly into prepared pan; bake until a toothpick inserted into the center comes out clean, about 20 minutes. Let cool completely before frosting.

8.Frosting: In a medium saucepan over medium-high heat, melt butter. Add sugar and salt. Cook, stirring constantly, until sugar is completely dissolved, then adjust heat to medium and boil 2 minutes longer. Add maple syrup and boil, swirling the pan occasionally, until sauce is thick, smooth, and coats a spoon, 2 to 4 minutes longer.

9.Pour hot caramel into a clean stand mixer bowl fitted with the paddle attachment. Beat at medium-high speed, scraping down sides occasionally, until sides of bowl are no longer hot to the touch and closer to room temperature and caramel is thick.

10.Add cream cheese, one cube at a time, until frosting is smooth.

11.Assembly: Pour frosting over cooled cake and even out with an offset spatula. Sprinkle frosting with fleur de sel (optional, although if going the pecan topped route it's even more important to do this to offset the strong sweetness of the maple). Top evenly with chopped candied bacon. Refrigerate if not serving within the day.

Maple Caramel Pumpkin Cake with Bacon Crumble Topping

Maple Bacon Caramel Corn

5 slices bacon

6-8 cups air popped popcorn

1 cup packed brown sugar

1/2 cup maple syrup or corn syrup

1/4 cup butter

1 tsp. vanilla or maple extract

1/4 tsp. baking soda

1/2 cup pecan pieces or halves (optional)

Preheat oven to 250° F. In a medium skillet, cook the bacon until crisp. Transfer to a plate, crumble or chop into chunky pieces and reserve 1-2 tablespoons of the drippings.

Spray a large bowl with non-stick spray and put the popcorn in it, along with the pecans if you're using them.

Combine the brown sugar, corn syrup, butter and reserved bacon drippings in a medium saucepan and bring to a boil over medium heat. Boil without stirring, swirling the pan occasionally, for 4 minutes. Remove from heat and stir in the vanilla and baking soda. It will foam up at first.

Quickly pour over the popcorn and stir to coat well, adding the reserved bacon. Tongs work really well for this! Spread onto a cookie sheet or roasting pan and bake for 30 minutes, stirring once or twice. Cool.

Makes about 7 cups.

Maple Bacon & Pecan Sticky Buns

6 pieces bacon, cooked, crumbled.

 1/4 C maple syrup

 1/4 C brown sugar

 1/2 C pecans, chopped

 1 tube refrigerated biscuits-such as Pillsbury Flaky Golden Layers

 1/4 tsp cinnamon

1. Heat oven to 350 degrees.

2. Combine maple syrup and brown sugar with pecans.

3. Stir in bacon and divide among 8 muffin tins of a 12 cup muffin pan.

4. Place biscuits on piece of wax paper and sprinkle with cinnamon.

5. Place biscuits cinnamon side up on top of mixture. Gently press to fit.

6. Bake until golden brown, 18-20 minutes. I suggest a baking sheet under it to catch drips.

7. Remove immediately and invert onto a baking sheet.

8. Let cool for 5 minutes and serve.

Maple Bacon Sticky Buns

Baker's Chocolate & Bacon Truffles

Ingredients:
6 slices Thick Cut Applewood Smoked Bacon
1/4 cup packed brown sugar
1/2 cup whipping cream
2 pkg. (4 oz. each) Sweet Chocolate chips, chopped
2 Tbsp. Butter, softened
1 Tbsp. Light corn syrup
1 pkg. (4 oz.) Semi-Sweet Chocolate, chopped

Directions:

HEAT oven to 350°F.

PLACE bacon in single layer on foil-covered rimmed baking sheet; sprinkle with sugar. Bake 20 to 22 min. or until bacon is crisp. Drain bacon on paper towels. Discard all but 1 Tbsp. drippings from baking sheet; reserve for later use.

BRING cream to boil in medium saucepan on medium heat; remove from heat. Add next 3 ingredients; stir until chocolate is completely melted and mixture is well blended. Crumble bacon. Add 1/2 cup to chocolate mixture; mix well. Freeze 1 to 2 hours or until firm.

ROLL chocolate mixture into 24 balls; place on waxed paper-covered rimmed baking sheet. Freeze 20 min.

MELT semi-sweet chocolate as directed on package. Stir in reserved bacon drippings. Dip chocolate balls, 1 at a time, in semi-sweet chocolate mixture, turning to evenly coat each ball. Return to prepared baking sheet. Drizzle with any remaining melted chocolate. Sprinkle with remaining bacon. Refrigerate 30 min. or until chocolate coating is firm.

Peanut Butter and Bacon Cookies

Ingredients:
2 cups Creamy Peanut Butter
1 cup white sugar
1 cup brown sugar
2 eggs
2 tsp. Baking soda
1/4 tsp. Salt
1 tsp. Vanilla extract
8 pieces of cooked Thick Cut Bacon

Directions:

PREHEAT oven to 350 degrees.

MIX Creamy Peanut Butter, sugar, brown sugar and eggs until combined in a bowl, usually about 2 minutes. Add in baking soda, salt, and vanilla extract. Finally, add in chopped bacon and mix thoroughly.

ROLL dough into small balls about 1 ½ inch. Place on cookie sheet lined with parchment paper roughly 2 inches apart. Gently press down using the tines of a fork making a crisscross pattern. Dip the fork in sugar to help keep it from sticking to the dough.

BAKE for 10 to 12 minutes until lightly brown. Cool on rack. Makes 2 dozen cookies.

Good Morning Sunshine Cupcakes

Prep Time: 15min
Total Time: 1 hr. 12 min

Ingredients:
3 cups wheat bran flake cereal
1-1/2 cups milk
1/2 cup pure maple syrup
1-1/3 cups flour
1 Tbsp. Baking Powder
1/4 tsp. Ground cinnamon
7 slices cooked Butcher Thick Cut Hickory Smoked Bacon, divided
2 eggs
1/4 cup butter or margarine, melted
 Frosting
4 oz. (1/2 of 8-oz. pkg.) Cream Cheese, softened
2 Tbsp. Butter or margarine, softened
1/2 tsp. Zest and 1 Tbsp. juice from 1 orange
3/4 cup powdered sugar

Directions:

HEAT oven to 400°F.

COMBINE cereal, milk and syrup in large bowl; let stand 2 min. Mix flour, baking powder and cinnamon until blended. Reserve 1 bacon slice. Coarsely chop remaining bacon; stir into flour mixture.

ADD eggs and melted butter to cereal mixture; mix well. Add flour mixture; stir just until moistened. Spoon into 12 muffin pan cups sprayed with cooking spray. (Cups will be full.)

BAKE 14 to 17 min. or until toothpick inserted in centers comes out clean. Cool completely.

BEAT cream cheese, butter, zest and juice in medium bowl with mixer until blended. Gradually add sugar, mixing well after each addition; spread onto cupcakes. Tear reserved bacon slice into 12 pieces; place on tops of cupcakes.

Bacon Brownies with Balsamic Frosting

Prep Time: 30min
Total Time: 1 hr. 30 min

Ingredients:
10 slices Bacon, cut into 1/2-inch pieces
1 pkg. (19 to 21 oz.) Brownie mix (13x9-inch pan size)
1 tub (8 oz.) Cream Cheese Spread
1/4 cup powdered sugar
1 Tbsp. Balsamic vinegar

Directions:

COOK bacon in skillet just until crisp, stirring frequently; drain. Prepare brownie batter as directed on package. Stir in half the bacon; pour into 13x9-inch pan sprayed with cooking spray.

BAKE as directed on package. Cool.

MIX cream cheese spread, sugar and vinegar until well blended; spread onto brownies. Sprinkle with remaining bacon. Keep refrigerated.

Maple Caramel Bacon Crackle

Prep time: 15 mines
Total time: 40 mines
Serves: 6-8

Ingredients
1 lb. bacon
1 package Pillsbury crescent rolls or store brand ones
½ cup maple syrup
¾ cup brown sugar

Directions:

Preheat oven to 325 degrees F.

Line a rimmed baking sheet with foil and liberally grease the foil.

Unroll the crescent rolls into one single plane of dough and pinch any perforations together to seal. Stretch the dough out a little with your hands so it's even.

Prick the dough all over using a fork. Set aside.

Cook the bacon. You don't want it to be fully crispy as it will crisp more when it goes in the oven.

Drain the bacon on a paper towel-lined plate. Chop or tear it into bit size pieces once it is cool enough to handle.

Drizzle ¼th cup of the maple syrup over the crescent roll dough.

Sprinkle with about ¼th cup of the brown sugar.

Top with the pieces of the cooked bacon.

Drizzle the remaining maple syrup on top of the bacon pieces, and top with the remaining brown sugar.

Bake for approximately 25 minutes or until bubbling and caramelized.

Remove from the oven and allow the pan to come to room temperature or warm to the touch before cutting or breaking into pieces.
You can serve the crackle at room temperature or slightly warmed.

It tastes best the day it is made, but can be eaten the next day if stored airtight.

Chocolate Bacon Bomb Pie

Prep: 30 min
Total: 30 min
Servings: 4

Ingredients:
3 cups pretzels (you can use whatever type of pretzels that you have)
2/3 cup sugar, divided
1 stick of butter, divided
1 package Fudge Stripes Dark Chocolate Cookies from Keebler or store brand (11.5 oz. size package)
12 oz. package of bacon, cooked and diced (1/4 cup reserved)
3 eggs
1 Tablespoon vinegar
1 Tablespoon flour
1/4 cup chocolate chips
1 can sweetened condensed milk

Directions:

Preheat your oven to 350.

Crush your pretzels and in a large bowl combine them and 1/3 cup melted butter and 1/3 cup sugar. Mix to combine.

Press the pretzel mixture into a pie plate and bake for five minutes.

In the same large bowl (no need to clean it out) crush your chocolate cookies. Now add the remainder of the butter (melted), the bacon (remember to save 1/4 a cup), eggs, the remainder of the sugar, vinegar, and flour and mix well.

Gently pour the mixture into your pie crust.

Top with the remaining bacon and the chocolate chips.

Pour the sweetened condensed milk over it and bake for 35 minutes or until the edges of the pie begin to turn golden brown.

Chocolate Maple Bacon Rice Krispies Treats

This recipe makes 2 dozen bars

Ingredients

For the Rice Krispies

3 tablespoons butter
5 cups Jet Puffed Cinnamon Bun marshmallows
1/2 teaspoon cinnamon
1 tablespoon pure maple syrup
1 teaspoon maple essence
1/2 pound bacon, cooked and crumbled into small pieces
6 cups Rice Krispies cereal

For the topping
1 bag (12 oz.) Hershey's Special Dark chocolate chips
Optional topping
1 teaspoon sea salt

Instructions
For the Rice Krispies

In a large sauce pan, melt butter and marshmallows over low heat. Stir until completely melted. Remove from heat and add cinnamon, maple syrup, maple essence, and bacon pieces. Stir until completely mixed.
Then add the Rice Krispies cereal.
Mix well.
Then pour the mixture into a greased 9 x 13 pan or a cookie sheet and spread it evenly with a piece of waxed paper.
Place in fridge to cool and set.
For the chocolate topping

Place chocolate chips in a double boiler (or a glass bowl that fits snugly over your pot) filled with water.

Bring water to a simmer on medium heat. Once chocolate starts melting, stir constantly with a rubber spatula until all chocolate is melted and had a smooth consistency.

Remove from heat and pour the chocolate over the cooled Rice Krispies and spread evenly with the spatula.

Allow the chocolate to cool a bit, then sprinkle lightly with sea salt if desired.

Place treats back in fridge to set completely.

Once the chocolate has solidified, cut into squares.

Chocolate Covered Pretzels with Maple Smoked Bacon Crumbles

Ingredients
1 bag pretzel rods
1/2 package chocolate candy coating, melted
1 lb. package maple smoked bacon

Instructions

Oven Baked Bacon Crumbles:
Line a baking sheet with aluminum foil.
Arrange bacon on the cookie sheet. You may not be able to fit a whole package of bacon on your cookie sheet. If so, have another baking sheet on hand.
Place the bacon on the center rack of a COLD oven.
<u>Do not preheat the oven</u>
Turn the oven on to 400.
Let bacon cook for 20-25 minutes or until crispy.
Chewy bacon won't crumble as well so we want to make sure it is truly crispy.
Remove from oven and transfer to a paper towel to cool.
Once bacon is cool, place in a food processor and process until bacon is chopped into large crumbs.
Transfer to a bowl.

Assembly:
Line your counter or a clean cookie sheet with wax or parchment paper and have your pretzels, melted chocolate and bacon crumbs ready to go.
Dip a pretzel into the melted chocolate and use a spoon to cover about 3/4 of the rod. Tap it on the side of the bowl to remove excess and place on wax paper to harden. Repeat.
Allow candy coating to harden for 3-5 minutes and then sprinkle on bacon.
Note: you do not want to let the chocolate get so hard that the bacon will not stick, but if you put it on while the coating is to wet the bacon will slide off.
I recommend doing this in batches of 6-10 pretzels, depending upon your pace, so you are not rushing to sprinkle on the bacon before the chocolate dries.
Repeat until you have used all your pretzels or until you have all the bacon covered pretzels you can handle.
Let the chocolate dry completely before removing from wax paper.
Store in an air tight container.

Apple Bacon Coffee Cake with Maple Glaze

280 grams all- purpose gluten free flour mix (or 2 cups regular wheat flour)

1/2 tsp salt

1 tsp Baking Powder

1tsp Baking Soda

2 tsp Xanthan Gum (if using Gluten Free flour)

1 stick butter, plus more for greasing the dish

1 cup sugar

3 large eggs, slightly beaten

1 cup sour cream

1 tsp vanilla extract

1 Granny Smith apple, peeled, cored, and sliced thinly

1/2 cup walnuts, chopped

6 pieces of bacon, cooked crisply and crumbled

1/2 cup brown sugar, firmly packed

1 tsp ground cinnamon

Maple Glaze

1 cup powdered sugar

1 Tbsp. milk

1/2 Tbsp. melted butter

1/2 Tbsp. brewed coffee

1/4 tsp Imitation Maple Flavor

A small pinch of salt

Butter a square glass pan and preheat oven to 350 degrees.

Chop walnuts and peel, core, and thinly slice the apple. Set aside.

Fry 6 slices of bacon until crisp, drain on a paper towel lined plate and crumble. Set aside.

In a small bowl combine brown sugar and cinnamon and set aside.

In bowl of stand mixer, mix butter and sugar on low until fluffy. Add beaten eggs in slowly until incorporated. Do the same with the sour cream and vanilla.

In a separate medium size bowl, measure out flour (using the scale if using anything other than regular wheat flour). Add in salt, baking powder, baking soda, and xanthan gum (if using). Whisk together thoroughly.

With mixer on low speed add dry ingredients to wet slowly until incorporated.

Spread half the batter in the pan. Arrange half the apple slices on top and sprinkle with 2/3 of the brown sugar/cinnamon mixture. Repeat.

Top with chopped walnuts and bacon. Bake for 50 minutes to an hour or until a knife stuck in the middle comes out clean.

Whisk together all the ingredients for the maple glaze and drizzle over the top of the hot cake.

Cool and serve.

Sunday Morning Maple Bacon Oozy Bread

1 package bacon, chopped (you can use pre-cooked bacon. This saves a step and tastes just as good)

1 8-ounce bottle maple syrup

1 stick butter

1 package of 8 refrigerated home-style buttermilk biscuits

Preheat oven to 350 degrees

Place a medium skillet over medium-high heat and add bacon.

Cook bacon until crisp, about 8-10 minutes and reserve.

Place a small saucepan over medium heat and add the maple syrup and the butter -- do not bring up to a boil.

Cook until butter is melted, then turn the heat off and reserve.

 Butter or spray a 3x9 loaf pan. Pour a couple tablespoons of the maple/butter sauce in the bottom (sprinkle some of the bacon on the bottom before adding the biscuits).

Layer 3 of the biscuits in the bottom of the pan. Tear up one of the biscuits and fill in any open spaces with the pieces.

Don't worry if any open spaces still remain, the ooze will fill those in as we progress.

Sprinkle half of the reserved bacon onto of the biscuits and top with about a 1/2 cup of the butter/syrup mixture.

Place the remaining biscuits on top, sprinkle the rest of the bacon over them and top with the remaining maple sauce.

Transfer to oven and bake for 25-30 minutes. When the top of the bread starts to brown, tent with foil allowing for the extra baking time without over-browning)

Remove and immediately turn over onto a serving dish.

Maple-Bacon Kettle Popcorn

This recipe makes about 4 to 6 adult sized portions

Ingredients:

4 slices bacon, cooked and grease reserved

1 tablespoon maple syrup

½ cup corn kernels for popping

¼ cup cooking oil (use the reserved bacon grease and add extra vegetable/canola/olive oil to make ¼ cup)

3 tablespoons granulated sugar

1½ teaspoon salt

Directions:

1. Fry the bacon in a skillet until brown and crisp. Remove to a paper towel-lined plate to drain and cool. Once cool, chop into small pieces and toss with the maple syrup.

2. Measure out the reserved bacon grease into a measuring cup. If you don't have a ¼ cup, add vegetable, canola or olive oil to make ¼ cup total.

3. Put the cooking grease/oil in a large pan and add the corn kernels. Sprinkle with the sugar and 1 teaspoon of the salt. Heat the stove to medium heat, cover the pan with a tight-fitting lid and wait until you hear the first couple of kernels pop.

4. Once the popping begins, use two pot holders to hold lid on the pot and shake the pot, then return to the burner. Continue to do this often throughout the popping process, every minute or two. This will help ensure that the sugar doesn't burn.

5. Once the popping is done, remove the lid and salt the popcorn with the remaining ½ teaspoon of salt. Use a large spoon to stir the popcorn. Pour in the bacon and maple syrup mixture. Toss together and serve.

Note If you have real bacon lovers ready to snack, you may want to double the amount of bacon and maple syrup in this recipe

Espresso Pound Cake with Maple Bacon Icing

Note - You can sprinkle your bacon with brown sugar before baking to make candied bacon for the top if you so choose

Ingredients:

1 1/2 cups all- purpose flour

1 tablespoons double dutch cocoa powder

1 1/4 teaspoons baking powder

1/4 teaspoons salt

12 tablespoons (1 1/2 sticks) butter, softened

1 1/4 cup granulated sugar

3 large eggs

2 teaspoons vanilla extract

1/4 cup strong espresso, cooled

1/2 teaspoon whole milk

3 tablespoons pure maple syrup

1/4 teaspoon maple extract

1 1/2 cups powdered sugar

8 strips center cut bacon, cooked and crumbled

Directions

Preheat oven to 350°F. Butter a 9 x 5 loaf pan. Line the bottom of the pan with parchment paper and butter the parchment paper as well. Set aside.

In a medium bowl, whisk together flour, cocoa powder, baking powder and salt. Set aside.

In stand mixer, beat together butter and sugar until light and fluffy, about 2 minutes. Add eggs one at a time, thoroughly mixing each time. Add vanilla extract and mix until combined.

Add half flour mixture and half espresso. Mix. Add remaining flour mixture and espresso and mix until smooth and no large lumps remain.

Transfer batter to prepared baking loaf pan. Bake for 55-65 minutes, or until toothpick inserted in the center comes out clean. Let sit until cool, at least 45 minutes and then remove from pan.

Then, in a small bowl whisk together milk, pure maple syrup, and maple extract. Add powdered sugar, whisking until smooth. Slowly pour on top of the cooled pound cake and sprinkle with crumbled bacon. Serve immediately.

Bacon Maple Marshmallows

Ingredients

The bloom

4 1/2 teaspoons unflavored powdered gelatin

1/2 cup cold water

The syrup

2/3 cup sugar

1/2 cup Grade A dark or Grade B maple syrup*

1/4 cup light corn syrup

1/4 cup water

1/4 teaspoon salt

The mallowing

1/8 teaspoon ground cinnamon

1/2 cup (about 1 1/2 ounces) finely chopped candied bacon**

1/2 cup Classic Coating, plus more for dusting

*The key to getting real maple flavor is using a dark amber Grade A or Grade B syrup, which are bolder than lighter Grade A varieties.

**To make candied bacon, lay 6 or 7 bacon slices on a wire rack set over a sheet pan lined with foil. Combine 1/4 cup light brown sugar with 1/8 teaspoon ground cinnamon. Rub over both sides of bacon. Bake at 350°F until deeply caramelized, 30 to 35 minutes. Let cool before chopping into bits.

Preparation

Lightly coat an 8-by-8-inch baking pan with cooking spray.

Whisk together the gelatin and cold water in a small bowl. Let it soften for 5 minutes.

Stir together the sugar, maple syrup, corn syrup, water, and salt in a medium saucepan. Bring it to a boil over high heat, stirring occasionally, until it hits 240°F.

You may need to lower the heat as needed as the syrup may bubble up.

Microwave the gelatin on high until completely melted, about 30 seconds.

Pour it into the bowl of a stand mixer fitted with the whisk attachment.

Set the mixer to low and keep it running.

When the syrup reaches 240°F, slowly pour it into the mixer bowl.

Increase the speed to medium and beat for 5 minutes.

Increase to medium-high and beat for 3 more minutes.

Add the cinnamon, increase to the highest speed, and beat for 1 minute more. Quickly fold in the bacon bits.

Pour the marshmallow into the prepared pan.

Sift coating over top.

Let it set for 6 hours in a cool, dry place.

 Use a knife to loosen the marshmallow from the edges of the pan.

Invert the slab onto a work surface.

Cut into pieces and dust them with more coating.

Bacon Maple Marshmallows Close Up

Bacon Maple Frosted Bourbon Cupcakes

Ingredients

1½ Cups Flour

2 tsp Baking Powder

1 Stick Salted Butter (room temp)

1 Cup Brown Sugar

2 Eggs

6 Tb Whole Milk

6 Tb Bourbon Whiskey

Instructions

Preheat oven to 350°

Sift together the flour and baking powder. Set aside.

In a large bowl, cream the butter and brown sugar. (2-3 minutes)

Add the eggs and milk. Mix until incorporated.

Add the bourbon and mix.

Slowly add the dry ingredients and mix until smooth.

Place liners into 2 cupcake pans. Fill liners 2/3-3/4 full.

Bake for 22-24 minutes. Or until light golden brown and cupcakes spring back to the touch.

Let cool in pans for 1-2 minutes. Then transfer to cooling racks.

Top cupcakes with Buttercream and Bacon

Maple Buttercream Frosting Recipe and Bourbon Maple Glazed Bacon recipe follow

Maple Buttercream Frosting Recipe for Cupcakes

Included is a plain buttercream base and then you can jazz it up if you wat to make it maple buttercream

Plain Buttercream

2 Sticks Salted Butter (room temperature)

3 Cups Powdered Sugar

For Maple Buttercream

Add to above recipe

6 Tb Pure Maple Syrup

Additional 1/2 Cup Powdered Sugar

Instructions

In a stand mixer fitted with the whisk attachment {the paddle attachment works too}, whip the butter for 30 seconds.

Add the powdered sugar 1 cup at a time. Scrape the sides in between each addition and start mixing slow then increase to medium/high. Mix for 30 seconds between each sugar addition.

(3 cups for plain frosting or 3.5 cups for the maple version)

Stop and scrape down sides. Add the maple syrup now if making the maple version.

(1-2 tsp of vanilla paste or extract can be added for vanilla buttercream frosting)

Mix on medium/high speed for 3-4 minutes. Frosting will be light and creamy.

Chill in the refrigerator for 5 minutes before frosting your cake.

Store leftover frosting in an airtight container in the refrigerator.

If making plain buttercream, heavy cream can be added to get the desired consistency. Add 1-2 Tb, 1 Tb at a time.   Makes about 4 cups.

Glazed Maple Bourbon Bacon

While this is used to top cupcakes, you may want to make a double batch so you can enjoy it by itself.

Ingredients

1/2 lb Bacon

2 Tb Brown Sugar

2 Tb Maple Syrup

2 tsp Bourbon Whiskey

Instructions

Preheat oven to 350°

Cut bacon strips in half. (optional)

Mix together the brown sugar, maple syrup and whiskey.

Transfer bacon strips to the glaze bowl and toss until evenly coated with bacon.

Line a baking sheet with foil and place a rack on top.

Lay bacon on the rack in a flat even layer.

Bake for 25-30 minutes or until crispy. Watch closely the last 5 minutes because the bacon will burn quickly)

Cool for 5 minutes before serving.

Bacon Monkey Bread

Ingredients

2 tablespoons butter or margarine

2 tablespoons real maple syrup

1/4 cup packed brown sugar

1/4 teaspoon ground red pepper (cayenne) - Optional

6 slices bacon, crisply cooked, crumbled

2 cans (8 oz. each) Dinner Rolls such as Pillsbury or store brand

Directions

Heat oven to 350°F. Spray pan with cooking spray.

In medium microwavable bowl, microwave butter and syrup uncovered on High 30 to 45 seconds or until hot.

Stir in brown sugar and red pepper until dissolved.

Stir in bacon.

Evenly spoon mixture into pan.

Unroll each can of dough into 1 large rectangle.

Cut each rectangle into 8 rows by 3 rows to make 24 pieces per rectangle (48 pieces of dough total).

Roll each piece of dough into a ball.

Arrange balls over butter mixture in pan.

Bake 30 to 35 minutes or until golden brown.

Cool in pan 5 minutes. Place heatproof serving plate over pan; carefully turn plate and pan over. Remove pan. Serve warm.

Bacon Caramel Apples

6 medium size apples
3-4 slices bacon
1 bag (11 oz.) caramels, unwrapped
3 Tbsp. water

Wash and dry the apples thoroughly

 Insert a wood or paper stick into the stem end of each.

Chop the bacon and cook it until crisp; remove with a slotted spoon to drain on paper towels, then crumble or roughly chop.

Reserve 1 Tbsp. of the bacon drippings and pour it into a small saucepan with the caramels and cream or water.

Cook over medium-low heat until completely melted and smooth.

Dip the apples into the caramel, turning to coat completely, then allow excess caramel to drip off and set on a parchment-lined sheet.

Sprinkle with bacon while the caramel is still soft, then let set.

Makes 6 baconly-delicious caramel apples.

Thank you for taking the time to read my Best Bacon Desserts. I hope that you find a family favorite or two in this book.

Sincerely,

Diana

www.ingramcontent.com/pod-product-compliance
Lightning Source LLC
Chambersburg PA
CBHW041221040426

42443CB00002B/34